The Only True Power Is in Connection

Pierce the earth
swollen, dark
and find the cool rock
worn by time's long breath.

Enter the breast
open, beating
heart's mysterious flower
warmed
by the coming of spring
and every moment's bursting.

1/25/92

Andrew K. Wilson

An early draft for Uncovering: A Spring Poem *that appears on page 23*

ANDREA K. WILLISON

The
Only True
Power
Is in
Connection

A Collection of Poems

1979 - 1997

WHITE WING PRESS

ISBN 0-9664706-0-5

White Wing Press
P.O. Box 1773
Schenectady, NY
12301

CONTENTS

Foreword

These brave and passionate poems are the work of
a generous heart and a quick mind. Andrea
Willison's beautiful volume shows a poet whose
belief is in the power of community and of language to heal, to join person to person and
thought to word. Over and over, these poems cre-
ate sparks of true vision in true language. In
"Orphan Poem for Francesca", the poet takes the
casual words spoken in conversation between
friends as a poem, and, when her friend will not
or cannot call them that, takes upon herself the
responsibility of writing her friend's poem with
her friend's words "...so she knows / that sometimes / when we throw away / a gesture, glance, or
poem, / there is someone / waiting quietly / to
catch it." That poem is, in a sense, an *Ars Poetica*, a
statement of Willison's poetics, or her sense of
mission as a poet: she is the one who will catch the
language of our experience and make poems of it,
make poems for us out of our lives.

"The Kiss" represents another mode of her
poetry, speaking for the connections with the nat-
ural world, with bark, leaf and tree. "I sat staring
through the dark / at the tree / and began to feel /
roots grow / from my toes / through the floor /
through the ground / till they touched the tree's."
She has a fine ability to summon a clear visual and
emotional equivalent of these moments of connection: In "Autumn Day" she paints the "color of
surprise / against a thin, blue shield / of sky, like
ice." Another powerful set of poems strung

through the collection speaks sometimes movingly and sometimes with a fresh, light-hearted wit and playfulness, of love between women. In "Contradictions" "a Butchy Femme sees a Femmy Butch / across a room". Even this light-hearted beginning, though, leads to emotional connection; by the end of the poem, the poet says "look inside yourself and you will find / the poem that was on my mind / the name of it is 'Being'".The magic spell poem, "Here I Am," in many ways a conversation with or parallel poem to Muriel Rukeyser's great poem, "Rune", lists "The sheet that wraps me / bear that eats me / … / noose that slips me / girl that hips me…" and powerfully comes to rest summoning up the "lover who wishes me / baker who knishes me / into being—and here I am."

Andrea Willison died young, and this strong volume is what she has left of her life, her mind, and her passion. Her poems speak all our lives into being, in intimate connection with the earth and with each other. Here they are. Read them.

Judith E. Johnson

Editor: 13th Moon: A Feminist Literary Magazine

to Grandma

one

I Thought I Heard a Drumroll,
I Thought I Saw a Carpet

———

I'm coming to my life late.
almost thirty years behind, dragging memories
like a ball and chain.

Many times I tried to cut the chain,
cutting my own flesh instead.
I wanted the lightness that comes when a pain is
healed after so many years
or a great weight is lifted.

Unlike Superman, there are few phone booths in
my life.
My transformations take long hibernations.

I thought I heard a drumroll.
I thought I saw a carpet rolling down.
But they were dreams.

I close my eyes, I lift the ball and chain
and step into the river. They don't drag me down
under the mud, but float instead,

and I tread water, padding slowly, toward the usual
red and orange sunrise.

I lift my long neck in the early morning breeze,
and flap my white wings gently.
The ball and chain are gone.

Published 1988
The American Poetry Anthology Vol.8, No. 5

The Journey
for Vera

———

Today
was a day with a grey wall
surrounding me
you came and said,
"You seem to be sitting on a lot of sadness,"
and the wall crumbled
crumbled from around me
until I had nowhere to stand
but in the safety of your eyes
so brown and deep.

We talked on
and you told me I was not alone
and then, finally,
you admitted you have a "gift" with people
you couldn't look at me
when you said it, as if you were ashamed.

But there's no shame in talent
and yes, you are an artist.
In the same way that a sculptor
or a painter shapes material,
you take a person's pain and hand it
back to her in a manageable design,
something solid she can hold
in her two hands.

For the past eight months
I have journeyed through your heart,
which is as wide as a river

and sheltered as a cave.
I have always been afraid of darkness
or that you would leave,
leave me alone
with only my own heart to hold me.

But darkness has not come,
in fact the walls of this place
are colored like stained-glass windows.
Sunlight shines through cracks in the ceiling,
showing our faces
two women travelling
our lives strapped tightly to our backs,
our bones as light as air,
together, and alone.

10/26/93

Orphan Poem for Francesca

"Life is like a peacock,"
she said,
"with all these different-colored feathers
to look at.
Since I met you
it's like a whole new kind of peacock,
with colors I have never seen,
is opening itself
before me."
I told her
she had just spoken
a poem,
that she should write it down
to save it,
but she pushed the poem away,
threw her words out the window,
would take no responsibility
at all.
So I am forced now
to pick her words up
from where she let them fall,
and I will let her read this
so she knows
that sometimes
when we throw away
a gesture, glance, or poem,
there is someone
waiting quietly
to catch it.

6/11/83

Uncovering: A Spring Poem

Pierce the earth,
swollen
dark
it's small green buds enclosed
and find the cool rock
worn by time's long breath.

Pierce the breast
soul's cushion
and find heart's stone
worn, too
with its beatings toward death.

Time pushes buds
to leaves
I see them
born perfect green (to their mother, the sky)
Death, you will wait awhile
for my heart catches
in awe of this
one moment's
bursting.

I wouldn't mind these poems that come to me
except they always start with words like wind
and free. They swirl inside before they hit the page
and try to lead me out of summer's cage.
But usually in fall I'm falling out of love,
I've gazed all summer long in someone's eyes
and at those starry starry stars above
until my mind has gotten lost among
the stars, and I've forgotten fall is just
around the bend, till suddenly it's here
before my feet can reach the ground again.
That's when the poems start to pour from me,
on wind and leaves and red and orange trees
as if my heart forgets that color is
not all it needs, that love takes work and time,
some effort to believe. But sometime soon
I swear, when I've been staring at the stars,
I'll pull my gaze back down to earth and face
the winds of fall before they blow away
whatever romance summer gave to me.
Then I'll be ready for those autumn poems
and won't mind words like swirling, leaves, and free.

Fall 1986

two

Sister Rituals

Judith, do you remember
        the eyelash wish?

cupped palm, breath blown whisper
        is it gone?

when we looked and saw it
in the palm of the other's hand
was the disappointment real?
wasn't the wish itself
the most important thing?

the touch of hands
heads bent together
in car's back seat
while adults in front seats
        backs straight eyes forward
didn't lift their feet over railroad tracks
        didn't hold their breath
past cemeteries
        didn't catch the falling eyelash

so many chances for a wish
        they lost

3/2/87

The Kiss

I never understood
how anyone could write
about trees—
stationary, predictable
trees.
I never understood
until one night
I sat on a window ledge
and saw
the new, green leaves
on the branches of a tree.

I sat staring through the dark
at the tree
and began to feel
roots grow
from my toes
through the floor
through the ground
till they touched the tree's.

When they did
a kind of energy
coming up through the tree
was flicked
from its leaf-tips
and floated
through the gentle air
to touch my face
like a kiss.
I remembered that when I was nine,

I kissed the bark
of the maple tree
on our front lawn,
because I knew
every branch by heart.

It had simply
taken those years
for the tree
to return the kiss.

Spring 1981

Weightless Again

I hear my father calling
from his mother's house
by the pond and the willow
the apple trees and tall grass beyond,
I see him standing straight,
by the willow
watching the light play
on the water, and his eyes
are blue, and his eyes

I climbed the willow quickly
I didn't look down
I wanted to prove
I could do it.
I stopped only
when I was higher
than I'd ever been
and when I finally looked down
I froze.
I knew I could move
if I really tried
but the next branch
was so far down
and I felt so weightless
when I moved my foot,
like a small balloon
caught on that branch
about to drift away.

My father climbed the willow
quicker than I,
he held up his hand;
I reached down
to give him mine,
and, like the string on a balloon,
my father pulled me down.

I hear my father calling
from his mother's house
by the pond and the willow
the apple trees and tall grass

I see him standing straight,
by the willow
watching the light play
on the water, and his eyes
are blue, and his eyes

Summer 1982

Connections

I touch the tree-tops
with my eyes,
landing lightly on one,
and then another,
riding the sun speckles
into the distance,
a rock skipped on water.
I remember when I was twelve,
and I wanted to give myself to the trees and fields
because I could not give myself
to people.
I watch the bird
and suddenly understand
that it is not flying
from anywhere or to anywhere.
I realize that no person
can remind me of these
connections,
only the bird.

9/12/80

Contradictions

a Butchy Fem sees a Femmy Butch
across the room
she smiles
and the other smiles back
they forget about each other
until the cold walls of a mental ward
bring them together
"Why are you so sad?"
"It's a long, long story."
"Do you see me going anywhere?"
"No," she laughs.
"Then tell me the story."
And she begins.

"My childhood was full of color,
rainbows everywhere,
music, poetry, my parents were artists,
though they worked as teachers.
I wrote my first poem at nine
and it went like this:

What is there to write?
For you must have felt
the same feelings as I,
and you must have sometimes found
the same reasons to cry,
I can't put myself on paper, though I foolishly did try,
but look inside yourself and you will find
the poem that was on my mind;
the name of it is 'Being'."

three

Recurring Dream

The rain hits
the windows
while papers rustle
and the office runs
smoothly on
talking, typing, brightly lit
while outside
it gets darker,
I stare at the rain and think;
"I am the same person
I was at eight, at fifteen, at twenty,"
it's a feeling
coming back to me lately,
in the office
on the subway,
in the shower,
I remember and remember,
like waking from a dream
only to forget
I was asleep
and then wake again
three weeks later
in the shower
on the subway
in the office, I wake
to remember
to shake the streamers
from the past
that sleep on my brain,
shake them
till they fall from my hair

and I say
look, I am moving forward
from who I was,
I am moving forward,
I am moving   forward,

Awake.

3/18/83

The Politics of Power

We were both women
both lesbian feminists
both working for the same agency
she the supervisor
I her secretary

I kept trying
to make these connections clear
I kept trying to show
that I was not a secretary
by profession that I was only there
because I had wanted to work
dressed in matching suits and skirts
she'd explain my work I noticed
when she pointed to mistakes
how thin and strong her hands were
they seemed disconnected
from the rest of her

on her coffee break
she'd talk loudly to co-workers
about what she planned to eat for lunch
she gained weight before my eyes
while I grew thinner
one morning I looked at her
all I could see was a pot-bellied
businessman
with a cigar

I tried to look at myself
to see what I'd become

but I was invisible
except when typing
it was then I knew I had to leave

since that day there's a scene in my mind
that keeps repeating
where I go back through those doors
walking quickly past the front desk
to the office where she sits
looking down into her face I say

Your power was never real
what I tried to show you
is that the only true power
is in connection
you could begin today
to try to touch another person
you have a place to start from
I've noticed that your hands at least are
beautiful

Technical Services Assistant at the
Graduate Business Library

Church steeples
rise outside the window
as they have every day
all fall and winter
Now white snow rests on top
of the black, sloping spirals

I sit at this desk again
typewriter and paper clips are
as they have been
every day
all fall and winter.

Now I am not filing
Now I am not typing,
changing the desk calendar
to tomorrow or
starting a conversation
with my co-worker
to show that I'm still friendly
and good natured, even after
having been here
all fall and winter.

Now I am writing a poem.
There is no one else here today
They will never know.
But two differences
will become apparent
Monday morning.

There will be more cards
to file and
when I sit with the others
as we work at our desk
typing, filing, labeling
they will all
remind me
of a poem.

1983

Aida

Aida sits every day
at the desk to my right,
filing slowly,
patiently, deftly.
"When you are heavy, like me,"
she said once,
"you cannot run,
even when you are late for work.
When I run, my heart, it beats—
too quickly."
She tapped the palm of her hand
to her chest.
Aida has been working for ten years,
she gets a three-week vacation
once a year.
She has a husband
and two sons,
"her boys."
When Miss Hewitt, our supervisor
is sitting at the desk
to my left,
Aida calls "her boys"
on her break
and speaks loudly to them
in Egyptian
so Miss Hewitt and I
will know
Aida has something
she will never
file away.

1983

If the Sunset Lasted

running through the city so as not to miss the sunset
people going about their business
they don't notice the orange sky
I reach my block   don't sink down
before I make it to the rooftop
take the stairs two at a time all six flights
I need to see something beautiful tonight
reach the sixth floor out of breath heart is pounding
unlock the roof's door
there it is
  blue sky

    orange streaked

heart slow breathing quiets
   orange spreads

    to tint the clouds

oh liquid sky pour through my head
and rinse these city blues away but
   orange starts to fade

    clouds   disperse

     sun is gone
I wouldn't need a lover
if the sunset lasted
all night long

1983

[44]

Monday at 5 PM, or, The Fate of a Poet Forced to Work with Business Librarians

I am blank
as the business books,
resting dumbly
on their shelves.
I am empty
as the sound of the rain,
hitting the windows
that frame nothing important.
My face feels as grey
as the fog that shrouds
the buildings rising high
outside,
but inside
the rumbling is getting louder,
threatening to explode—
to destroy this blanket
numbness;
My hot volcano of
a heart is tired
of other people's snow
falling on it.

1983

New York City's First Sign of Spring

the bums
on fourteenth street
smooth   their greasy hair

put their coats   on the ground and
settle back,
crazy referees   waiting to see
what the new season brings

Spring 1983

East Village Sunday Morning
for Pat

There is a lightness
that we touch, in passing,
in the morning
walking
past the junkies smiling;
in their hands
are breakfast pills
and you buy some
in the morning,
in the winter sunlit morning,
and we each take half, hoping
we can slow,
we can slow,
the morning down.
We sit on a bench
in the park's filthy morning
and the cold
feels so good, to the bone.
And the lightness
flits between us,
when you blink
it leaves your lashes,
when I speak
you watch my mouth
and you kiss me
and you taste it
and the lightness
flits between us
in the winter sunlit morning
and it, oh, feels so good,
to the bone.

1/82

Recorder

turning pages   grey and smooth
with names of people
I don't know
typed across the top
they're all students
at the Graduate
Business School
and I am a "Recorder"
recording grades
name changes
new address forms
conversations
a person's face   the joke they tell
recording   what I have to buy
on my way home
plans for my future
yes there is a reason
why I have to make it through
this day
why I have to keep
reminding
myself
that every name I read belongs to a real person
who could possibly
at any moment rise from the page
three-dimensional and
multi-colored
ready to dance with me
out the window

up to the sky
with a color so blue
it has never been
recorded

1983

As Autumn Comes

As autumn comes,
the city opens
to the wind and leaves
with quiet gratitude.

We will not suffer now,
moving sluggishly
from room to room.

We will put our jackets on,
turn up our collars,
and hurry past each other.

Secretly we notice
how beautiful the sky is
when the air is finally clear,
like a blue china bowl
wiped clean of dust, it sparkles.

We sparkle, too
our eyes are brighter
we quicken to ourselves
and remember
there were things we had wanted
from the summer.

Will we find them now
that the air is crisp
and our pace is quicker?
There is little time
for wondering.

When the wheel turns
we will turn with it again,
we must let our thoughts ride
on the cool wind of Fall
while our dreams swirl around us
like the leaves.

How will this season find us?

When the city's frozen
and our heels click loudly
and echo
through the hollow streets,
when we pause
to watch black smoke
curling upwards
to an ashen sky,
will we think of summer?

Or will our hearts turn also,
all the way around
to face the changes in ourselves
that mark our lives

like the red splash of paint
on the bark of a tree,
that marks a cold hard trail
in winter.

Fall 1983

Kim Joquoy's Song

Your voice gruff
from twenty years of cigarettes

I heard you from the office
almost every morning

standing on the front steps
of the boarding home for disturbed adults

staring every passerby straight in the eye
and singing

the words didn't matter—
what you meant every time
was Goddamn it I might be crazy
but I can still sing

1987

Unsettled in New York City

I am gathering the days,
the little happenings of life;
I am fingering my worth—
change for the bus to work,
keys to the new apartment.
I am feeling my way in this new city,
etching her phone number, her smile
onto the map of my waiting brain
where it is hungrily absorbed.
I have stopped listening
to the people who ask,
"Haven't you lost weight?"
(What a surprise,
considering that I climb five flights
to load the fridge with
half a paycheck's worth
of groceries,
that will be gone within three days.)
I am listening instead
to the
Yes
beat of my heart

Yes
I am living in this one-room furnace
writing this poem
with sweat dripping down my face
and no I don't feel sorry for myself,
because I will read this poem
two weeks from tonight

to a room full of women
who may have gone for weeks
without anyone telling them
Yes
you can
change the world,
in between cooking supper
and doing laundry
and going to poetry readings.
They may have heard only,
"What? You live where?
You're getting a degree in
Women's History? Creative Writing?
You'll never get a job

Why don't you get married?—
or at least switch to computer
engineering
Let the President worry
about the chances of nuclear war."
But women know
the daily chore
of revolution
won't wait until tomorrow.
So I will look at all of you
when I read this poem,
and gather your faces
like shiny beads to wear
around my heart
and the next time
someone asks me
when I'm going to settle down

I'll smile
and tell them:
"When there is
no hunger,
no racism,
no sexism,
no heterosexism,
no nuclear weaponry,
no war of any kind,
no poverty,
no injustice; then maybe
I will settle down."

But till then
I will live in my one room,
work 9 to 5,
go to demonstrations
and poetry readings.
Still sometimes
in between doing the dishes
and rushing to class,
I have wondered
if this is all for nothing.
As if in answer,
I have felt a sudden energy
flow from my head to my toes.
I like to imagine
this energy comes from some woman
living 500 years from now
in a world of peace and equality,
who senses me doubting,
and looking back through the years

she smiles, and places her matriarch's
hand
on my back, to urge me
gently forward.

Summer 1982

four

Silence, for My Friends at Southampton College, 1977-78

my first year in college
I slept with a man
so I wouldn't be a virgin
all my life
so no one would suspect
anything
but I shouldn't have bothered—
my roommate went looking
through my dresser drawers
and not knowing what
she would find
found it anyway   a book of poems
one for every woman
I was in love with

I wondered why
she started putting that blanket up
between our beds at night
why six other people
who had been my friends
wouldn't talk to me
the rest of that
first year
I went a little crazy
so that even when a woman
finally kissed me
I couldn't feel it
for a long long time
I was listening still
to their silence

well I   have   changed   since then
and not   because anyone helped me
but because I decided
to go on being myself
no matter how much hatred
it brought me

there have been many kisses
since that one I couldn't feel
many poems   published
I read the love poems now   out loud
hoping they're heard
by every woman
searching secretly through dresser drawers
for something she must suspect
lives in her own heart
why else would it be the one thing
she's so afraid of
yet looks so hard
to find?

Fall 1988

Unspoken

On the street
men's eyes
ring like registers,
calculating my worth—
from head to toe,
like merchandise
they already own.

"Hey baby," and I
keep my eyes
straight ahead,
face bland
no encouragement,
but they don't need it,
they say,
"Come on,
I know you like it,"
I want to scream,
"No, I don't like it,
don't like your eyes
hot on me
like a brand.
like dirty flies,
would like to poke them out,
would like to spit in them;
that I would like."
when I am late
for a train
and running
through Grand Central;
a man

(he does not know me)
sees me and says, loudly,
"Take it easy, baby,
but I like that bounce."
I search my mind
for something I
could have said
to make him feel
the way he
made me feel
but it doesn't exist
in any language
and I'm left alone,
running on
trying to pull words
from air,
like sponges
to soak up my rage.

Summer 1981

Flight of the Challenger

you went to bring back information
instead   you exploded   leaving
a strange trail   of white smoke
making sure we understood
anything can happen

you weren't   (as the papers reminded
afterwards)
an astronaut
what were you doing
strapped to that chair
pushing against
the bulky uniform
layers of metal
surrounding you
straining   to   be   free
of the ground

you knew
the preparation began
long before you were chosen
with the way you lived   willing
to take chances
you taught children in a small town
who looked to you
to show them life
from different angles

this was your reward
to be a student

who would view the earth itself
from another angle

finally   you're moving exactly
as you knew you would
closer to and farther
from everything you've ever known

did you see or hear anything
that told you you were about to die?
or did it happen without warning
your soul continuing   on the journey
even while your body
and the metal one it rode in fell away
even while your parents' faces
began to register horror   captured forever
by the cold lens   of a television camera
they saw your life ended
          that alternate route   taken
by a shuttle
heading not toward any star or sun
          but sideways to some other place
                    where they couldn't see you
anymore
          where they could only see   the path you took

you thought of them
in the instant
before the explosion
and hoped they would know
the path you were about to leave
with its beginning and end
was an illusion
because in that instant
of violent flames

[64]

you were already moving slowly
through the hole
left by your disappearance
into a quiet place
where you touched the cool surfaces of planets
and drew
with your astronaut's hand
an infinite   infinite   equation

Revelation

A rose
is a rose is   a rose is   a rose is
a rose is a rose is a rose is a
rose is a rose is a rose is a rose is a
rose is a   rose is   a rose is
a rose is   a rose is a   rose is a
rose is a   is a
rose   is a rose is   a rose is

we think humans
are great philosophers
but if we listen carefully
we'll hear
what crickets have been telling us for years

For My Brother

"Dear sister,
I wake in the morning
to flies on my face
and dress quickly
in my soldier's uniform.
I eat a bowl
of cold cornmeal
then hurry with the other boys
to stand in line
so I can learn to shoot a gun,
at tree-stumps now, but later—
boys like me.
I am proud to learn to shoot—
they killed our mother
and our little brother.
I will kill them for this.
Don't worry for me, sister,
I am not afraid to die,"
he writes to me.
He is only twelve years old
and I believe him.
The last time I saw him
was one year ago.

We were at the camp
in the forest,
we got up early in the morning
when the birds were singing,
so we could say good-bye.
The sun shone through the trees.
he told me he would see me

in America,
took the ring from his finger that reads
"Viva la revolucion",
and gave it to me.

I wanted to scream at him,
to tell him he was only acting macho,
but I knew he wouldn't believe me
no matter what I said
so I hugged his skinny body to me
told him to be careful,
gave him the money I had hidden.
Then I left him standing there.
I could see him as the helicopter rose.

He looked so small, and never wiped
away
his tears.

The letter said,
"Dear Rosa,
Your brother is
the bravest of them all.
Two days ago
we were attacked
by rebel forces.

Our captains wanted to test
the younger ones
and asked if there was someone
brave enough to run to the mountains
and bring back extra soldiers.
Your brother volunteered.

He was on his way back
down the mountain
when the rebels found him.
I can hardly bear to tell you,
but they shot him in the back
as he ran.
I know how you must feel—
you are his sister.
But I wanted you to know
we won the battle,
all was saved because of him, the bravest of them all
and my best friend."

All was saved except my brother's life.
Now the anger
that was in his words
the day I left
is burning in my heart.
Will you tell your president:

Yes, yes you are right.
I was born in North America
I speak only a little Spanish
I am a poet
Not a Nicaraguan soldier girl.
I have a mother and a father and a sister
I never had a brother
and now he is dead.

Dangerous Gift
for H.N., singer & political activist

————

I. Opening

In every person
who is fighting
there exists a secret weapon.
Whether it is in their eyes
in how they look at life
or in their words
which may form poetry that heals
or in the strum of their guitar—
through which they tell their story
or in their fingers—
which may sign so gracefully;
this weapon it exists
in some form or another.
But never till I met you
had I seen it in so pure a form.
You open your mouth to speak
and particles of light
dance in your voice,
you sing—
and particles come together,
liquid lightness traveling
richness swelling
in your lungs
delicious sound you give to us,
pours to our ears like honey
and sweetens the pain
of life that we are living
Yet it doesn't always

feel so sweet
to open to this sound,
for you don't ask us
what or whether we want to feel;
you grab us with your voice
and it can hurt
to open to the words
that you are singing
but we have no choice
so as the song begins
our cautious hearts are waiting.
Your gentle voice
caresses them,
then suddenly we're with you,
we're with you in your pain
the pain you feel at loving
in a world that's full of hating,
the pain we feel at living
in a world so full of death,
but now we're here together
and life is all that matters.

II. The Song

You have given us the music,
for their freedom without violence
your voice an instrument
an instrument of light
that has traveled quickly to us.
We are caught up in its ray
and our voices join together,
you have led us through our pain
into this sound of joy.

You have pulled from us a song
that we'd hidden in our brains
You have showed to us a song
that's as deep as the earth
You have opened up a song
that's as wide as the sky
This is my song to you
in the form of a poem
and when I read this poem
it will be your song they'll hear
for your song it has a name
that can be spoken many ways
for your song it has a name
that you have learned to say with beauty
for your song can be a poem
or the light in someone's eyes
it can be an old man dying
it has been too many dying
for their country or their people
it can be a people fighting
for their freedom without violence
it can be two women loving
it will be all of us
someday.
You have given us a gift
in the form of a song
but this gift we cannot keep;
we must keep giving it to others
You are just one person singing
in a land where death is breeding
but our chorus has begun
and it echoes
You have given us a song

we had been afraid to sing
but your voice is strong and steady
as it leads us
You have given us a song
and when we sing this song together,
when we take it for our own,
then this song it has a name
as it flows through us towards others
then it cannot be contained
you can trust your song with us;
we will take it for our own
and call it power

The Women Who Couldn't Stop Kissing

the women who couldn't stop kissing
were in love
the women who couldn't stop kissing
became children in eachother's arms
the women who couldn't stop kissing
became one another's mothers
the women who couldn't stop kissing
saw a world of rainbows in eachother's eyes
ran their fingers through eachother's hair
and laughed
tasted honey on eachother's tongues
and loved that sweetness
the women who couldn't stop kissing
were getting even with a cruel world
the women who couldn't stop kissing
were drawing thorns from eachother's hearts
the women who couldn't stop kissing
had hands that couldn't stop touching.
had breasts with nipples like berries.
had legs like wild swans.
were glad they were not men.
the women who couldn't stop kissing
poured like water into eachother
until the darkness washed away

7/3/91

five

If The Moon

If the moon were your face
and the night your embrace
I'd kiss the darkness
and tell the sun not to rise

Si la luna fuera tu cara
y el noche tu abrazarra
besaria la oscuridad
y le dejera sol que no subiera

10/86

The Way Out

Kissing you
is like all the old clichés
seeing fireworks as
I feel the earth move under me, while
your lips are soft as rose petals and
violins play in the background.

Kissing you
is also like
jumping off the top of a train
doing 80 miles an hour
knowing that even if I don't land
in the alligator-infested water
on both sides of the tracks
it's still 100 miles
back to civilization
I've never been here before
and you refuse to give me clear directions
insisting I find my own way
as the alligators crawl
slowly toward me
their broad smiles dripping
and I stumble backward
into the open arms
of a headhunter.

Well, fine, who needs you, anyway?
I will climb a tree
and swing from vine to vine
screaming for the wild animals and natives
to get out of my way
dropping coconuts on monkey's heads

then when I see you
staring up at me
eyes wide, mouth hanging open
in surprise because
your plan didn't work and
I'm not wandering lost in your jungle
I will laugh
and sweep you up with one hand

and we will sail
through the red and the yellow
of your sunset jungle sky
high above the snapping jaws of alligators
to some real place, together.

10/15/82

The Annointing
for Dinah

———————

Like a cathedral
you took me in
washed me of innocence
gave me colors
to look through
bathed in your light
I became a child again

like a story
our lives continue
your eyes still light my way
leaves clear from my path

I regret the nights
we will not lie together
wrapped in each other's darkness
cleansing each other
in silent water of darkness

we gave each other fragments
a watch, three rings, some songs
things to cling to in a storm

the storm is raging now
I see you reaching for me
wind whips hair
around your face

hands touch
waters clear

[80]

we sit in a small place
and talk of tears

I kiss the water
on your face
you question why I love you
ask what's the hidden reason
I wouldn't tell you then
but now I will:

You are cleansed by light
and the power to heal.
You are the gentlest of women
and your touch is holy.

12/91

Thorn

When you kiss me
a light sweeps through
the darkness of my mind
reminding me of everything
I used to know
my mother's cool cheek
as she kissed me good-night
my father's hand holding mine
as we climbed a mountain
the feel of grass on my face
when I was a child and lay
next to the cool, damp earth;
your body comforts me.

and when your hands touch me
their gentleness reaches deftly in
to a place in my heart.
it is a dark place
but the light from your hands
spreads through my heart like water
slowly easing my desire
and loosening a thorn
I never meant to grow there.

2/91

The Test

Your eyes
glowing green
from your deep brown face
hold the friendly comfort
of fields of grass
or seas
where I could float
supported by the salty,
shifting brine.
I have seen comfort
in other eyes before
promises of floating,
buoyant.
But the current changed.
Their waters flowed away
from under me,
and I would have fallen
had I not learned quickly
and with flailing arms,
how to float on thin air.
So I will study your eyes,
noticing
when you look toward the
window
if the light splinters
those seas of green
in more than one
direction.
And when her eyes,
gold flecks in blue

so close to me
on the green, green, grass,
when they look at me
and then dance away,
to search the trees and sky,
why don't I reach
to touch her cheek,
bring back
her dancing eyes?

And when her eyes
dark brown like mine
question me
from across the room,
her voice asks,

"How long have you
hated your father?"
while her eyes ask,
"Will it be soon
that you put your
arms around me?"
Why don't I rise
and cross to where
she sits in her
black, swivel chair,
look down at her
till she rises, too,
put my hands
through her soft black hair?

Why do I answer the question
that is spoken aloud to me,
yet the one that hides
in someone's eyes
I don't know how
to answer.

6/14/83

How to End a Political Argument
between Two Dykes

That night in bed
I told you the reason
I march in demonstrations
with women, screaming
and crying with rage
is so I can wake the next morning
cleansed of this rage
and ready to love;
you told me
you had decided that
I hate men.

You told me the reason
you don't march in demonstrations
is because you're not a
"group person",
you'd rather be with
one person, loving them, instead of
shouting your feelings
to the world.
I said, "that's valid",
while I wondered
what you're hiding from.

You thought
for awhile,
and then proclaimed,
"The difference between us is:
You want to die on the cross,
and I just want to do the twist."

At that we laughed,
and since you're beautiful
when you laugh
I kissed you,
and as we kissed,
you forgot
your next argument,
and we both remembered
what it is we
have in common.

10/26/82

The Words I Never Said

wind
rushes into a heart
that was filled
with the smile you left
in a doorway
before you turned
to go
without ever tasting
the words I
never said
that sit in my mouth now
like bitter dead bugs
I swallow them daily
I wash them down
with maybe
what if
might
have
been

9/2/87

Marta's Voice

Your body, tall and wide
crowds a room when you enter,
commanding attention.
You can never be anonymous
even when you want to.

You are a square peg
trying to fit
in the round hole
of your life,
trying to make the hugeness
of your wants
shrink to something
someone can accommodate.

You fumble, moving
like a blind person
who refuses not to run.

And when you trip, and fall
in the dark
why is there always someone there
to help you take your blinders off,
to shield your eyes
till they can stand the light?
I think it is because
they see in you
something that moves
effortlessly, just
beneath the surface,
that finds it's way out

now and then
in a glance, a word, more often
when you sing
with a voice that flows
as you cannot,
a voice beginning deep
in your flesh, your blood
that rises slowly
through your lungs,
upwards to your heart
where it is pumped with effort
to your lips
and then explodes,
powerfully
easily,
as if the best parts of yourself
were finally freed
and flying gracefully
through the air.
To have opened, suddenly
to you,
the marsh land
of your eyes, hazel and soft
in the harsh
morning light they drew me in those months ago
and I have let myself
get foggy in their sweetness,
to have opened, suddenly
to this,
and now to close again,
as suddenly,
leaves me aching
my body grows scales that blister

without your ointment,
my mind catches on sharp thoughts
crisp, cold, they hurt
without your laughter
to smooth the edges.

You are the one who laughs;
I crawl inside myself.
When will another person
laughing,
draw me slowly out?
Never?
My heart gasps,
opens its red hand of need,
its grasping fingers feel around
and come back empty,
whisper to my body
of long nights and
crisp, cold thoughts
cutting me
to tatters

Just one more kiss,
your tongue like an icicle
inside my burning mouth,
and I would let it melt me
so far down this time,
I wouldn't notice
you were gone.

2/8/83

Highway Bandit

When I met you, you carried your past,
the weight of mistakes on your back.
You showed me each one, proved we couldn't last
then put them all back in your pack,
looked on down the road and spotted another
who'd help lighten your load for a while,
said, "Let's be friends since I've got a new lover,"
and turned away with a smile.
I stood for a while, unable to move,
trapped in the freedom you'd left me,
when the wheels of anger put me in motion,
I let them turn till they'd swept me
on down the road until I'd passed you,
now you cry from behind, "Wait! I can love two!"

Where to Meet a Lover Instead of at a Bar, Party or Political Convention

Where tattered terrestrials gather on playgrounds
built secretly underwater,
and slowly rising
this is where I want to meet you

where snowflakes fall and whisper to horses flying
through the sky
where carriages have one wheel and are faster than
the speed of light
this is where I want to meet you

where moon doggies hide in their desert holes
where sage brush blows across the empty fields at
night
and spirits gather for seances to conjure up the
living
this is where I want to meet you

where rainbows fall continuously stumbling over
garbage to reach us where we live
not in palaces but ordinary houses and streets
except that here people touch each
other all the time
healing scars with the flick of an eyelash
this is where I want to meet you

where hollows form in the trunks of trees and echo
through forests of billowing leaves
where music plays from each tiny stem
a light shines from inside every blade of grass

and over rolling hills so green it hurts to look
at them
this is where I want to meet you

where the past and future overlap
we become transparent taking the form of eagles
flying over adobe homes
landing in cities with messages wrapped in our
talons
this is where I want to meet you

at the point in my mind where sound and light
rush together
and form this vision of a place where thoughts are
heard far from their beginnings
where everything is possible
and love is the standard sought after law
that courses through the channels of our veins
no matter where we came from
this is where I want to meet you

1987

Whispers
for D.D.

———

Today,
we were not together
but I felt you in my heart,
when someone smiled at me.
Today,
we were not together
but I saw you in the shimmering petals,
falling from a tree.
And although we were not together,
when I read a poem
I heard you in the silence between words
and I knew with certainty
you were whispering, "I miss you,"
in a soft and gentle voice to me

Dreaming Awake

I know exactly
how the light
slants across the ceiling
of my room
in the night

I've heard exactly
how the children call
to each other while they play
in the street, summer, winter, fall,
it doesn't matter,
they keep calling to each other
in the night, for they belong
more to the streets
than to their mothers.
I've seen exactly
how their faces look,
thin and hard
bright eyes that dart,
they are wise,
I know exactly

I know exactly
what the men say
to each other in the night,
outside my window,
they are calling each other
when the children
are all finally in bed,
they are calling to each other
so that everyone will know;

they are men and they're allowed
to walk the streets at night

I sit in my bed
and stare
at the factory across the way,
I know exactly how the lights
will go out, one by one,
lights will flicker
like the patterns in my brain,
and I'll sit in my bed,
looking out
at the now darkened windows.

I know exactly
how the light
slants across the ceiling
of my room
in the night
and I think to myself
how none of this would matter
if only I could know
exactly
how it feels
to have your body
next to mine,
to let the night take form
in the rhythm of our breathing
as we ride each other's bodies
past the children calling,
and men telling stories,
past the night-time shadows
on the walls

then I could see exactly
how your face looks
when I touch you,
how the lines melt away
from the smooth, dark skin
around your eye
and your mouth forms an o
through which comes the pleasure
in your moans,
I want to hear exactly,
and I would let you take me
to the place inside myself
where I could feel your passion
beating hard against
and I would open to it,
we would become the night
with all its night-time voices
your face like the surface
of the moon above my body,
you touch me with your eyes
then with your mouth,
see your face shine down
like a gentle moon
on the only part of night
I can bear to see exactly
the hollowed silver brilliance
of your soul.

Conversation

we were sitting
in that cafe you chose
where they don't serve liquor
though I always wish they did
when we are there together
I couldn't stop nodding
at everything you said
I thought if I concentrated
hard enough
I wouldn't notice
that your eyes
didn't match your words
that as you moved
the scent you always wear
washed over and through me
my desire rising to meet it
your eyes softened then
their question answered
your words stumbled over each other
and we saw
for a moment
the part of one another
that flutters
in the space
between our words

The Accusation

My life
is a fiery orange need
as my heart
explodes
like a small volcano
in my chest;
I want to destroy
everything I love.
I can't bear
this need for you,
as if in your veins
flowed juices
I need to survive,
addicted
as an alcoholic.
If I pretended
not to love
how you breathe
when we make love,
or how you move beneath my hands
as if you danced
to the beat of my heart—
or how you live your life
like a question mark
I can only answer when we lie skin
to skin together.
If I pretended hard enough
I could deny your existence,
or I could simply suffocate you
in your sleep
so I wouldn't have to feel

I wouldn't have to
feel
this angry fire
in my chest;
How dare you
have the nerve
to love me.

Bird

you are a bird
scratching softly
at the door to my heart
scratching softly
with your tiny claws
with your desires
held in your beak

if I let you in
you will flutter flutter
search my soul for seeds
eat what you need
and fly away

On the Train

On the train to New York
we did not kiss
we did not put our heads
on each other's shoulders

I watched a heron
dip its body
on the water and then rise.

When we got to the station
I knew exactly where we wanted
to go and how to get there
you were impressed
since its been 5 years
since I was here.

First, I showed you
the five-flight walk-up
across from the factory—
I loved it there.

Then we walked
down Greenwich Ave
into the heart
of the village.
I asked if you
would hold my hand

You said no.

I showed you NYU Law School,

where my grandmother
taught law
for thirty years.

The man there remembered her,
said she was
the "female equivalent
of a gentleman";
found a picture of her in a yearbook,
and copied it for me

I showed you where she used to live
before she died
felt sadness—but not despair.

We ate at a diner
down the street,
complaining about the slow and smelly waiter.

Walked up to Astor Place,
to the Institute for gay and lesbian youth,
The place you want to work
when you finish your degree.

I waited in the lobby for you, watched a parade of
queers go by.
Wasn't sure if they could tell I'm queer, too—
took off my jacket so they could read
the "Up & Out" T-shirt I had on.

After half an hour
I was inundated
by gay teenagers—boys

who kissed each other on the lips
sat down next to me
and started talkin' bout
"girlfriend" this, and "girlfriend" that,
and "Did you know she's got a lover now? Can
you believe it?"

They glanced at me,
not sure if I was friend, or enemy.
I smiled, trying to show I was no enemy,
but they were too busy, or too paranoid, to notice.

By the time you came out,
I felt anxious and tired,
and sad, that we queers have to live
with so much fear.
But then we met Gloria,
our new-found friend
and she showed us all
the gayest places.

Ate supper in a Mexican restaurant
you two talking politics,
until you said something personal
"Well, I have school and a beautiful lover,
why do I need money?"
I loved you for saying that,
still do.

Saying good-bye to Gloria was hard
she'd told me earlier she has no social life.
But we told her to call us,
before we get together

for the 25th Anniversary of Stonewall,
the first gay riot—the first time queers
stood up to the cops—
the men hitting back with their heels,
the women with their muscles.

Managed to get on the earlier train,
even tho it said "By Reservation Only"
The woman who stamped our tickets "OK."
said not to tell anyone
she was the one
who'd sent us to an already-overcrowded train.
You smiled at her
and she smiled back at you—
"She looks pretty when she smiles,"
You said as we walked away.

So do you, my love, so do you.

On the train back
we didn't kiss
we didn't hold hands
but I put my head on your shoulder
while I slept.
It was enough.

5/18/94

six

Hike
for my father

---

the hike I took today
reminded me of those I took with you
when I was young
there was something about the way the light fell
through the branches of the trees
the way we stopped to look at everything
one person explaining rock formations
another pointing to a woodpecker
and looking it up in their bird-book
reminded me
of how you used to explain everything
even when I was too young to care
not just rocks and trees and birds
but philosophy and politics
history and literature
you were always pushing me to learn more
there were a few years when it worked
I got straight A's and earned your approval
but then came the teenage years
when it wasn't cool to care about anything
except lip gloss, eyeshadow, and boys
when I didn't respond to your discussions
of politics and theories
you got angry and we fought like hell
each trying to free ourselves
of the need to go backwards
to return to the way things were
only in the last few years
have the pieces come together
now I join in your discussions

of the world
a world that is also mine
and I am grateful to you
for making sure I stopped
to think, to analyze, and discuss
but most importantly
to look at the way the light falls
through the branches of the trees.

Words to Keep You

Mother,
when I see you
I feel a bursting
in my chest
that pushes my words
up and out;
I want to tell you everything,
"I read my poetry the other night,
I hate my job,
I'm learning how to love,
I'm living here, in New York City,
alone, your daughter, living."
Mother,
it hurts
to look in your brown eyes
and know I will not look in them
until my own eyes
close forever;
it isn't fair—
you brought me up,
you loved me till I loved you
and now you will not promise me
you will always be there.
You were supposed to be
immortal,
but there are lines
around
your eyes
that weren't
always there
Sitting in a cafe

as you look at me
gently, overwhelmed by this person
your daughter
I know
I love you too much.
When you're
not here anymore,
I will sit in cafes alone,
and, surrounded by people talking,
faces close together,
glasses clinking,
I will have to keep spouting
my words
to the air.

10/28/82

The Death of Fannie J. Klein

why can't I feel
anything but numb
when I think of her
lying in that hospital bed
a green mask on her face
a tube in her arm?

yesterday I stood
in that room alone
wishing there was someone there
to help me look at her
but it was only she and I
and she was sleeping

so I looked out the window
at the city and the river
helicopters landing on the pier
a seagull flying by

so much space but she and I
were stuck in that room
I with the helplessness
I felt before her coming death
she with the heart
that's failing her

why can't we leave our bodies
during life
to become a speck of blue
in the pattern of the sky
or a seagull or some dust

on a helicopter's runner?

why does it have to be in death
that we leave?
by then it's too late
to return to the body
to tell it all the secrets
we've learned from the sky

does she feel this, too
as she lies so dignified
among the tubes that feed life to
her
in doses much too small
for her impatient heart

or is she gone from her body
though her chest rises and falls
perhaps she's left me for a while
trapped here in this room
while she's out there soaring
with the bird

My Father's Eyes

In the frozen blue lake
of my father's eyes
his dreams   like sequined fish
bat their heads
on the dark   underside
of the place   where his vision
froze   cold as ice

when I look in those blue pools
I feel a cold pain
begin in my stomach
and rise to my throat
where it stops
the words I would say
to him if I could
if he could hear me
if we could be far away
from the expectations
he was supposed to meet
and didn't   and never will

if we could be far away
sitting in a field
of tall grass and blue sky
maybe he would stop
feeling guilty
for all the things
he didn't do
maybe he would forgive himself
for not after all

being able to dive deep
inside himself
through murky waters
to the bottom to search there

for a sign something to tell him
he was on the right course
before the wind and rain
dragged him down would he find
jewels glowing in a wood chest
gold coins in a burlap bag a starfish
something he could bring

with him back to the surface
to hold proudly in his clenched fist
wet and dripping high
above the water
something so beautiful
that he would understand
he does not have to justify his life

After My Grandmother Died

After my grandmother died
my mother and I looked at each other
for the first time realizing
we wouldn't always be alive
together   I saw her as she is
a whole person with faults and weaknesses
with many strengths   her love of life
her gentleness   her willingness
to understand   my need to be
myself

she told me
she had been standing   on the deck of a ship
with a railing just in front to hold on to
to keep her from falling in the ocean
she told me
her mother was
that railing

I want to tell my mother
who's afraid now of falling   I think
there really is no ocean
just a huge space made up of hearts and spirits
of people we have loved who have arrived before us
but I guess   she already
knows this

what can I tell her
to make her feel less empty

mother

you have always been my railing

For Jackie

when I look at you
I see
strength bursting from your body
your legs that won't carry you
are beautiful as your face—
chiseled in stone
yet delicate
as a child's
your eyes are a wide sweet blue
which
when I look into
I feel myself carry you
while the flowing dress you wear
envelops us
your eyes show me too
a young girl running on strong legs through a field
where caterpillars crawl
Your mother stands in the doorway
watching
the girl's golden hair
flying behind
her four-year-old
daughter is running toward
polio
running toward
a motionless life
running toward pain
locked tight now inside your woman's breast for years
like a chrysalis
that dreams of wings

(which if I could truly carry you)
would open and bloom
at last.

10/2/89

December 14, 1996

And she held my head
and she rubbed my hair,
And she sang me a song,
and asked me to tell
her what was wrong
And she held my head
and she rubbed my hair,
and she brought me
back, from who knows where.

seven

Reasons

I've turned around
so many times
now I'm holding on
to anything
that will keep me going straight ahead
I think the next time
I turn around
the dizziness will kill me
what gives me reason to hope
I won't spin so fast next time?
a child's eyes
conversations over the phone
the fullness of a night
sitting quietly
sipping wine   with her
strength and anger
grown inside me
after denying myself the joy
of these things
for so long
for no reason.

11/18/79

The Truth

My mouth opens
and words come out
yellow green blue splatter
talk talk   talk
yes   yes I'm fine
no I'm not afraid
I can talk to you
and smile, and move my arms and head
just like a person
who knows
she will be just fine
and the more I talk and talk and talk
and nod my head oh yes
yes yes yes yes yes
fine fine fine fine fine
the more you will believe it
but what if when you turned to go
I grabbed your arm and said
what I really feel right now
is that I need someone
to put both hands upon me warm and strong
and hold me till I'm still
You would run—
and so I let you go.

A Lack of Communication

You do not seem to understand:
My insides are made of bits of glass
that move when I walk and
scrape the sides of my stomach.
When I try to talk to you,
my voice, resonating
makes the glass fragments jump
and stick to the sides
of my lungs and throat
bleeding me slowly back
to silence.

Some Women's Eyes

Some women's eyes
have in them
something
I am afraid to try to name
I have seen it
mostly in women's eyes
so brown,
so dark and so deep
the woman herself
doesn't know where this
brown darkness ends
and where she begins.
The woman knows
that people see
in her eyes something
that draws them to her
People speak to her,
and she watches carefully
their eyes, their lips,
searching for some clue
as to what they see.
Even as she does this,
she listens to the
person.
She hears what they say
not only with their
words,
but with the tone of
their voice,
with their movements,
their hands,

their eyes;
she is opening
herself
as they speak
and their feelings
enter her.
She is as powerless over this
as they are.

When the person
who is talking senses that the woman
is listening to them
not just as others do
but with her whole being, the person is filled with
                                                    gratitude
which shines from their eyes like a light
as they look at her

The woman, seeing this person's happiness—
not knowing it exists because of her,
thinks to herself,
"How empty I must look to this person
who has so much life inside
that it must spill, shining,
from their eyes."

The sadness the woman feels from this mistaken
thought
becomes part of what the other person
sees in her
And the person realizes that the woman's eyes,
though beautiful, are blind;
she cannot see herself.

10/17/82

Untitled I

suddenly everything is brighter
        a pair of sunglasses left on for years
and now removed everywhere I look
        I see the world shine
I am as big as the sky
        and as wild as the wind
when it changes direction
        my life begins now
all things will come to me
        and I am finally ready to let them

The Professional

certainly I can pay you
fifty dollars per half hour
to help me handle my life
which I have to live
for free
why don't you just charge
according to number of words
per minute
and raise the price
if I start
to cry
while speaking?
of course I will pay for my last
appointment
because I missed it
without giving you 100 hours notice
and you have a waiting list of clients
20 pages long
food? clothes? shelter?
I don't   need them
I must use every penny
to pay someone to tell me
why I think   the way I do
come to the school of social work
learn how to use your degree
as a mop   for the blood
of those who need you

Dr. Kevorkian

Dr. Kevorkian
I'm sick of all this shit
Life, I mean
I'm about to throw a fit
Pain, pain, pain
and then some more
if life were my customer
I guess I'd be a whore
So Dr., Dr., I need you
I want your needle and
I want you to
Gimme some of the everlasting sleep
I wanna go low and I wanna go deep
Gimme some a yer white hot death
Gimme your drugs
and I'll give you my last breath
I'm twirling up and down a merry-go-round
But the horses aren't real
and their feet don't touch the ground
I see myself reflected
in other people's eyes
but instead of my real self,
all I see are lies,
It's a soulless journey
and my heart's been mutilated
so take my aging body
I want it refrigerated
I wanna come back
in a thousand years
when it's safe for children, women,

Blacks and Queers
to walk the streets of their own country
without cringing in fear.

Religion

Across the milky sky
are terrible tears cried
by the one who died for us
they say
they tell us, love him.
love him. love.
the man who died
to save us from our sins.
And I do
see his face sometimes
in times of sorrow.
But he is not the person
whose hand I reach for
when I'm lonely
surely a hand so ethereal
would offer little comfort
Jesus you offered
to save us from our sins
but a mistake is only a sin
when it can't be forgiven
I forgive my mistakes
I forgive them
I turn them into silver stars
and place them in the sky
where they show me the long and lonely trail I took
to gain this ragged
independent heart

10/23/89

Words, Like Swallows

Where is the man
with a message in his palm
if not a drop of blood
then at least a sign
that he has suffered

with light in his shadowed eyes
if not a beam
then at least enough
to see my scars

with a mouth that speaks
words to my ears
words like poetry
poetry like birds
birds like swallows
to flutter
in my empty heart?

1/26/90

Watercolor Life

the lines
in my mind are melting
red and yellow
smudging
like drops of rain
the walls around my brain
are crumbling
leaving pebbles sticking
to the paths of cells
that criss and cross
behind my eyes
if I can let this happen
without clutching
at the fragments
as they shift then
        I will wear
        new patterns
        in my head
        new colors
        that swirl and flow
        a watercolor life
        oh let me learn
        to change

Drop of a Tear

inside the drop of a tear
are small bacteria
that live inside our bodies
just as we live on earth
an infinitesimal part
of the universe
Why then
does my pain
feel as big as a country

I have visited this country
too many times
with no visa   no way to get home

I'm on dry land now
and I steer the course of my life
This boat is small but strong

I will push myself past
icebergs, rotting logs and weeds
I will steer around rocks and crevices

Anyone who wants to pass can
but I won't save the ones
scrambling to get on board
Get your own boat own world
own life
I can't save you from the storm
I can only save
myself.

The Woman

the smoke clears
after the fire is put out
my dog and I see
in the distance
water ripples
on the lake
under the sun's touch

the woman
is not with me now
but I see her eyes
in the water's silky rings
and her smile
in the rising sun.

2/8/97

The Return
for Jones Home

This place
whose rainbows healed me
fills me with lightness
people come here
to recuperate
many are old, most are broken
all are cold, even frozen
standing outside, looking through cold glass
at their lives.

Here we begin to heal,
to escape from something
which weighed our days
and cut us with sharp thoughts
at night.

Here we find ointment
in the laughter of others
and gentle guidance,
salve for our wounds.
We are split apart
so the warmth of the world
may enter again.
We are terrified, but open.
We cringe at every touch.
The mind awry isn't just a disease,
It's putting your heart to the heart
of the world
and feeling too much.

3/14/92

I Am Whole

So now I've made it
past the probing doctors
and comforting nurses
past the constant counseling
and the rules and regulations
so now I've made it
back to a safe mind
filled with light and warmth
instead of frightening monsters
back to health
except for mild anemia
the price I'm paying
for pushing the limits
of this mental health system, designed
to keep us sick and dependent
not prepared for our humanness
to coalesce again
a ball of mercury
splintered
and then whole
I have left behind the sedentary life
of the mentally ill
the waiting for someone else
to push me into motion
the panic that paralyzes and numbs the mind
I am free
and whole
as a rock
strong and still
whole
as a wave

constantly moving
whole as a voice
strong and steady
I will always love those
who I leave behind
but I am whole as the heart
of a fluttering bird
as I leave my fetters,
useless and limp,
on the distant ground below.

6/3/92

Words Like Diamonds

Lately it seems
I slip into my skin
as if into a costume
laced with fringes,
inlaid with diamond stones.

I finally know
exactly who I am
I know
down to the bone.

I dance
and the music carries me
I am an Indian
become an eagle
flying for my life.

I love
and the warmth
pours through me,
I am a lover
with rainbow hands that heal.

I write and the words are gems,
inlaid on the page,
I write and the words are 'regalos',
gifts from me to you,
I write and the words are fire,
that scorch the edges of the page,

that burn inside my heart,
until they leap
the invisible horizon,

And sear
into your soul.

eight

Starting Over

I.
Starting over
with less than before
is hard.
More time's gone by,
more mistakes,
more wondering,
if I'll succeed.
I'm older,
tired.
It's not a game anymore.

II.
But I know what I have to do;
I'll gather all my child dreams
and the ribbons which
flow from them.
I'll feed my mind
with these liquid thoughts
till they burst from me
in colors
to flow and rain on everyone
and carry me farther
from where I've been.

For the Wolf

they say the wolf
will lick his blood
from the sharp-edged blade
until his tongue is gone

he wants to leave
no part of Self
no juices
for the Hunter

if he could turn
and walk away
though his blood shines
on the blade
he'd live to howl
again

I want to kneel
on the bloody ground
to lift his tongue
from the leaves
and sew it back inside

I want the blade
with the shining blood
to pierce my frozen
Hunter's heart.

11/28/88

Cocoon

floating
on my bed   a tomb
high above   reality
from darkness   to dawn
waiting   for the end
wanting   not wanting
to be saved
not thinking of why
I had to escape
why she didn't fit
in my self-constructed
perfect   world
finally   phone calls
a pill   and sleep
but first   colored images
to comfort me
into dreaming
fearfully knowing
in the morning
I will rise
leave my dried up shell
on the bed
and slowly learn
to fly again

Fall 1979

Waves

Noise subsiding
    gently riding
        the waves of this life

Sometimes sorrowful
    often joyful
        mostly full of love

for the here and now
    for the possibilities
        for the potential

    hidden

inside a bud
    on a tree
        in a cautious, gentle
            spring.

3/31/94

Resolution

you are inside my heart
like a cold stone
you are my rock
you are my home
you are inside my heart
like a red rose
I will win
I cannot lose
I will hold to what I have
I will ride
the changing waves
I will not let
sleep take me
I will let
love and anger wake me

2/2/94

Untitled II

Where is the life
I remember being promised—
the one I heard about in whispers
from my mother's lips that
traveled backwards down her throat,
through her blood and into mine?
I squatted in her stomach, head cocked, listening
and I grew strong
fed on those whispers,
strong and sure that soon
I would dive
from between her legs
into a world
that was prepared
for me to land.

Life, Like a Truck

life's comin' at me full speed ahead
I'm standin' still watchin' it bear down
like a diesel truck with a driver whose been drinkin' beer
and listenin' to Dolly Parton
he's got a two-day old beard
scruffy hair
callused hands
blood-shot eyes
and probably a lover
waitin' in Wisconsin
I don't know if he'll stop for me (I've screwed up so
many times before)
but if he doesn't
I'm sure as hell gonna grab the bumper and
ride that ramblin' truck
on down the yellow line
called life.

11/8/89

Cloud-Woman Poem #2

Cloud-woman
knows the meaning
of mystery
knows   when the sun
breaks through the clouds
it's not always a sign
of love
knows even sparrows sing
with death
in their tiny throats

but when she sails
through midnight skies
of rose petals and green leaves
she forgets   the danger
until a hawk's wing
brushes against her cheek
she veers away
reminded   once again
this quick but casual movement
is the only way   to win

Cloud-Woman Poem #3

the cloud-woman's hair
grows like cotton candy
over her cunt
Spanish moss
under her arms
willows
from her head

I've never seen her
but I've loved her
all my life

she would heal me
if she could
but her skin
is as delicate
as the white lid of sleep
on a cat's eye and

if she touched me
it would shed
like a snake's
slowly   painfully

red blisters would appear
on her fingers
on her arms
she would not scream
but would rise up to the clouds again
to rain blood on my head
as she died

die if you have to
but heal me   cloud-woman
with your delicate hands
of sky

1/1/88

Untitled III

Do you know what it means
to drift so far from yourself
that you have to catch
the next boat back?
But sometimes the rower
charges more
than you can afford
so you stand on the shore
trying to remember
how you came
so you can swim back
the same way
but the current
has changed.
Before I jump in again
I'm going to make damn sure
my life-jacket is full of air
because I'm sick to death
of seeing pity
on their faces,
as they glance behind
leaving me
swallowing mouthfuls
in their wake.

2/4/80

Black Sheep
for Emily Dickinson, Anne Sexton, and Sylvia Plath

The quick-slime toad
of punishment has me
by the fucking toes
it shakes me so fast and then says,
"that's the way it goes."
Well, shake me toad
I don't care
because your mouth is a purple bruise
from which come devil's words
I've heard them all before

I've heard them all before
the shit that from your mouth does pour
oh what a tasty dish
you say, regurgitating on your fish
it's interesting; your vomit
has particles of blue, like Comet

oh frog of sin
oh frog of death
you pester me till I'm near death
you try to make me love the line
the dotted one
in Highway 9
the one that leads to suicide...

Oh Esther Green
of Plath's Bell Jar
that name again,
as black as tar

Call me crazy if you must
Do—
Violate the patient's trust!

call me crazy if you will
call me fucked up
screwed up, still
you need me
for your little games
you feed me, need me
I'm to blame

I'm to blame
for all your sins
just look at the mess
my life is in
I'm to blame
that your life is sad
that your mother
always made you mad

NO, SYLVIA
NO, ANNE, MY LOVE
I won't wear those bloody gloves

I will wear this life instead
it doesn't fit, it wants me dead
but I will wear this life instead
and turn the steeple
on its head

Anne, you never found the breast
to give you peace

to give you rest
I found it once
then watched it leave
I gave myself
some time to grieve

but you, impatient as you were
the space it left the emptiness
was your mur   der

A Queen—Without a King—
as Emily would say
A Bride—Without a Ring—
A Sparrow—Searching for a Crumb—

Oh, Emily
you lesbian
forced to be a Puritan
Say it now in your timid voice,
Reach your genius Self
across the years
give your breast to Anne
the Hungry Dear

the one who couldn't
get it right
who counted stars as eyes
in the middle of night
she lay down like you
upon a bed
in a snow-white gown
with a veil on her head

She Lay Down Aching—
On the Bed—
She Cut Her Self—
And There—She Bled
She Lay Down—
—Naked—
On the Bed—
She Married It—
It Fucked Her—Dead

Holy Trinity

Sylvia
I've wanted to write this poem
for years
five to be exact
if I must be exact
and you were always so exact
as if you had taken a knife
and drawn the edges of your life
on the pale skin of your wrists
as I did then

Virginia
You hide behind your words
as if they were veils
covering
your many faces
the masks you wore
to hide your wild self
the self that entered
the water
parting the waves
going inward
to your own irrhythmic
soul

Anne
I love your name
you saw the stars
in your lover's eyes
her freckles
were the universe

but you counted and counted and counted
until what you counted
became lost to you
the softness of a breast
a lover's kiss
you gave away for awards
of respectability
you gave your voice
your body
your poems and finally
your hands.

You three
are the Holy Trinity
I pray to
when I realize
I'm alive
even after
the night on the highway
when I opened my own veins
to the darkness.

Here I Am

The sheet that wraps me
bear that eats me
breast that teats me
noose that slips me
girl that hips me
mouse that squeaks me
Arab who sheiks me
hose that leaks me

friend that kisses me
person who misses me

lover who wishes me
baker who knishes me
into being—and here I am.

10/21/96

nine

Endings

I saw the day for the first time
touched lightly over regrets
that had burned, before.
Felt the freedom acceptance brings
the strength
to make a new beginning
with boundaries
wide enough for mistakes
strong enough
to forgive them.
Endings.
A purple sentence across the sky
with the sun at the end, period.

12/17/79

Autumn Day

with trees orange-red,
the color of surprise
against a thin blue shield
of sky, like ice.
Autumn day
half hollow
as a pumpkin.

9/27/81

The Lit Path

Above the wide margin of the sky
flashes of light appear like warnings
I watch them
hold my head back
catch the rain in my mouth when it falls

Ready for sleep
eyelids close
flashes of light appear
I watch them
symbols in my dreams

I heard a voice singing
flashes of light crashed in her eyes

Now, alone,
I watch sparks strewn across the future
lighting a desperate path
where conversations,
death,
flashes of light
will follow

1987

The Sound of the Sun Going Down

Lying on the couch
at dusk,
I closed my eyes
and listened,
straining to hear
the sun go down.
Instead I heard the sky
singing one note—
blue and clear,
heard the trees' green
humming as they grew,
heard someone dying
in a far-away small room,
heard brown and hungry children,
and children laughing, too
heard people making love,
heard every being's voice
sing from each cell
of the earth's brain
their sounds together ringing
like a bell in my chest,
too heavy for my heart to hold—
until the sun, in the middle,
going down,
pulled the quiet
from the center
of each sound
until all that was left
were their echoes
floating up
to the darkened sky

The Journey II

I.
When I first started out
I didn't know the road would be so hard
or that the walk would take so long
exhaustion overtaking me
long before I got there.

I didn't know the face I saw
would be my own
staring with incomprehension and tears
a face filled with horror
for tomorrow.

I threw the stone up in the air
the one with "courage" imprinted on its side
and it landed in a strange place
neither here nor there.

I started walking but I lost the stone
with "transformation" written on its side
the most important one; I lost.

Yet now when I look at the faces,
I see hope, the beginning of rebirth
a place to start from — you are my sister,
you have a heart like mine,
riddled with the bullets of time.

II.
So take my hand, sister, and I will lead
you back towards the world

where heartache exists but doesn't have to
color everything we say:

Are we speaking?   Are these words
we caress each other with
or just stones with an idea inscribed,
one more thing to interrupt
our lives.

No, these are not just stones
This is a way to communicate
You've seen it done and so have I
Healing can come with the blink of an eye.

Hold me close in a realistic embrace,
one that holds room for me to grow
one that shows us the roads we're on
and if they don't lead in the same direction
we'll say good-bye before we start.

Tell me someone! Say to me,
"The water will recede leaving shiny stones
of chipped auburn and polished blue
each one with the message,
All things will come to you;
for you're finally ready to let them."
This was a promise I made to
myself, years ago in a land
of abundance, before I knew the smell of poverty.

Before I knew the smell of poverty
could wrap itself around you,
become a comfort, an old blanket

wet and clammy, stuck to the skin
like a Peter Pan shadow.

III.
But new promises come to me
whispers like twigs
from the Oriole's nest
build something
as solid as steel,
flexible as water.

I'll build something—
a platform to stand on
where everyone will see me
colors emanating from my heart
rippling like waves.

Come to me, come to me,
Rocks, seaweed, empty crab shells
bottle with a ship inside
I will toss you all into the sky
and you will
arch in a rainbow
allowing me to cross to the other side
where life begins. *

IV.
The tide
offers everything I've lost
the ring you bought me,
the jewelry that was stolen,
the cat who died.
all the years when all I did was cry

I stand as my life washes over me
bringing back everything
  everything
my life never really existed
my life will endure forever
what's the truth
I wonder as the hand of the ocean strokes my cheek
whispering, "Love,
you have a long way to go
before you understand
what's real and what's not
you have miles to travel
on a moonlit sea
before love means more to you
than pearls."

8/27/97

* *This verse, in the original manuscript, is marked "take out".*
We have chosen to include it.

Andrea K. Willison was born in Williamsburg, Virginia in 1959, but grew up and lived much of her life in the Capital District of New York. Graduating from Sarah Lawrence College she lived in New York City for three years, writing plays, fiction, and poetry. Andrea wrote poetry through-out her life, some published in various journals and collections. She played the guitar and drums and set some of her poetry to music. Andrea worked in human services, while advocating social change; she was particularly concerned with the rights of women, gays, and lesbians, and people with mental illness. Known for her compassionate friendships and her tenacious humor, she was sensitively intellectual and a dedicated student. At the time of her death in 1997 she was working on a Doctorate of Arts in Humanistic Studies from the University of the State of New York, Albany.

Heartfelt acknowledgement

is offered

to all who loved Andrea,

To our friends and to our partners; Martha for her support, Tom for everything, and Barbara Zimmerman for her love and hard work on this collection.
And to Joel Haycock, Carl Lehmann-Haupt, Helen MacDonald, and Pat Testo.